THAT'S OUR TEACHER!

The author and photographer would like to thank all the many teachers, administrators, other faculty members, children and parents at P.S. 87, Manhattan, for their inspiration and generous cooperation in the making of this book. Special thanks to Stephen Brown for all his wonderful help and support in the preparation of the manuscript.

Library of Congress Cataloging-in-Publication Data
Morris, Ann, 1930-
That's our teacher!/Ann Morris ; photographs and illustrations
by Peter Linenthal.
p. cm.—(That's our school)
Summary: Introduces Lisa Shlansky, an elementary school teacher,
describing what she does during the school day and how she
interacts with other staff and students.
ISBN 0-7613-2373-2 (lib. bdg.)
1. Teachers—Juvenile literature.   2. Teaching—Juvenile literature.
[1. Teachers.   2. Occupations.]   I. Linenthal, Peter, ill.   II. Title.
LB1775.M697   2003
371.1—dc21   2002152486

The Millbrook Press, Inc.
2 Old New Milford Road
Brookfield, Connecticut 06804
www.millbrookpress.com

THAT'S OUR SCHOOL

THAT'S OUR TEACHER!

Ann Morris

Photographs and Illustrations
by Peter Linenthal

The Millbrook Press / Brookfield, Connecticut

Our teacher is
the best. Her name
is Lisa Shlansky.
She teaches us
many things.

She teaches
us to read . . .
and to write.

Sometimes our
teacher takes us
to the library
to hear stories.

Sometimes
she takes us
outside to read.
That's really fun!

Our teacher teaches us
to count and to measure.

Sometimes she shows
us how to cook.

She teaches us
to make all
kinds of things.
Look at the
tiger we made!

Our teacher helps us learn about the world from top to bottom. She shows us where places are on the globe.

She teaches us about animals and nature. "Look through the glass," she says. "What do you see?"

She teaches us about plants. "Smell the flowers," she says.

Our teacher is always very busy
making things happen. She plans
our lessons and checks our work.

Sometimes she talks with our parents on the phone or in person to let them know how we are doing.

Our teacher
helps us
when we're
feeling good.

And she helps
us when we're
feeling bad.
We can go
to her with
any problem.

Our teacher often sits
with us at lunchtime.

Once we made
tacos for lunch.
"Taste the taco,"
she said.
She loves doing
all these things.
We do, too . . .
and we love her.

Our teacher likes to have fun with us.

She also likes to
visit with the
other teachers
in our school.

Our teacher
is also a mom.
She has her
own family.
Her husband's
name is Arnie and
her children are
Max and Olivia.

 They all eat breakfast together before they go off in the morning.

Our teacher at three years old

Our teacher (left) at ten years old

When our teacher was little she loved school and worked very hard. When she was a little older she wanted to be a ballet dancer.

Our teacher at twelve years old

Here's our teacher at her high school graduation.

After high school, she went to college to become a teacher so she could help children learn.

Here comes the bride!

Here comes the family!

After college, our teacher met her husband,
Arnie. They fell in love and got married.
Then they had their children.

Now they live close to our school.

Once we were out at the market

and there she was.

"THAT'S OUR TEACHER!"

THINGS TO DO

Would you like to know more about your teacher or what it is like to be a teacher?

Would you like to do something nice for your teacher?

Try one of these activities.

Be a Teacher

- Take turns being the teacher in your classroom. Teach your class something you want to share with them that they may not know about.

- Be a teacher to some younger children in your school, or to a younger brother or sister. Read to them. Explain something new that you have learned.

Learn More About Your Teacher

- Interview your teacher. Find out why he or she became a teacher. What special things did your teacher have to do to become a teacher? Does your teacher like being a teacher? What is the best part? What is the worst part?

- Ask your teacher what school was like when he or she was young. Did your teacher like school? Ask your teacher to bring in photographs from his or her school years—class photos, plays, school celebrations, sports teams, graduation.

Make a Book

Surprise your teacher with a class book.

Include drawings and a special message from each of you.

Make a cover for the book, and bind the book together with yarn or string.

A parent or a student teacher may be able to help you.

About the Author

Ann Morris loves children, and she loves writing books for children. She has written more than eighty books for children, including a series of books for The Millbrook Press about grandmothers and their grandchildren called *What Was It Like, Grandma?* For many years Ann Morris taught school. Eventually, she left teaching to become an editor with a children's book publishing company. While she still sometimes teaches workshops and seminars for teachers, Ann Morris now spends most of her time writing. She lives in New York City.

About the Photographer-Illustrator

Peter Linenthal is a talented photographer and illustrator. He studied fine arts at the San Francisco Art Institute. He is a native of California and teaches at the San Francisco Center for the Book. Peter Linenthal also loves children and working on books for children. He did the photographs and illustrations for Ann Morris's books about grandmothers.